Introducing MOZART

ROLAND VERNON

Chelsea House Publishers
Philadelphia

First published in hardback edition in 2001
by Chelsea House Publishers, a subsidiary of
Haights Cross Communications. All rights reserved.
Printed and bound in China.

First published in the UK in 1996 by
Belitha Press Limited, London House,
Great Eastern Wharf, Parkgate Road,
London SW11 4NQ, England

Editors: Claire Edwards
Designer: Andrew Oliver
Picture Researcher: Juliet Duff

3 5 7 9 8 6 4

The Chelsea House World Wide Web address is
http://www.chelseahouse.com

Library of Congress Cataloging-in-Publication Data applied for.

ISBN: 0-7190-6041-1

Picture acknowledgments:
AKG London: front cover, back cover bottom, title page, 6 top, 7 top, 8 bottom,
11 bottom, 12, 13, 16 bottom, 17, 18, 19 bottom, 23 bottom, 24 bottom, 25
bottom, 27, 28. Bildarchiv Preussischer Kulturbesitz: 26 bottom.
Bridgeman Art Library: 8 top, Chateau de Versailles/Lauros Giraudon,
16 top Mozart Museum, Salzburg, 21 Historisches Museum, Vienna, 23 top
Kunsthistorisches Museum, Vienna. By Permission of the British Library,
London: 24 top. J. Allan Cash: 7 bottom. Donald Cooper/Photostage:
19 top, 22 bottom, 25 top. E.T. Archive: 6 bottom, 17 bottom. Mary Evans
Picture Library: back cover top, 22 top. Ronald Grant Archive: 26 top.
Scala: 11 top.

CONTENTS

INTRODUCING MOZART

SOME COMPOSERS are best at writing music for instruments, others for voices. Some write best for the stage, others for church. Some composers do their best work when they are young. Others achieve nothing great until they reach middle age. Wolfgang Amadeus Mozart had it all. He was a master of every type of music he wrote. He was a child star, one of the greatest pianists of his generation, and, by the age of 20, the most exciting composer in all Europe. But the world at the time was not ready for his genius, and he spent most of his short life searching for a job. He died in his thirty-sixth year, at the peak of his powers but penniless. This was a tragedy, and yet Mozart wrote more music in his short career than many other composers who lived far longer. He has left behind more than 600 extraordinary works.

DI FIGARO,
O SIA
LA FOLLE GIORNATA.
COMEDIA PER MUSICA
TRATTA DAL FRANCESE
IN QUATTRO ATTI.

DA RAPPRESENTARSI
Nel Teatro di Praga

IDOMENEO.
DRAMMA
PER
MUSICA
DA RAPPRESENTARSI
NEL TEATRO NUOVO DI
CORTE
PER COMANDO
DI S.A.S.E.
CARLOTEODORO

BIRTH OF A GENIUS

Leopold Mozart (1719–1787) was born in the German town of Augsburg, but moved to Salzburg as a student in 1737.

Leopold and Anna Maria Mozart lived in the Austrian town of Salzburg. Leopold had a good job as a composer and violinist at the court of the prince-archbishop who ruled Salzburg. Of their six children, only one had so far survived—a daughter, called Nannerl. But on the cold morning of January 27, 1756, they had their last child, a boy. They called him Wolfgang. Leopold described the baby's arrival as a "miracle from God," because he seemed too small and weak to survive.

Musicians in those days were servants of rich and powerful people, but Leopold was a well-educated man. As well as working for the archbishop, he became a respected violin teacher and published a popular book on violin playing. Leopold was determined from the start that his son would also be a musician. But he cannot have dreamed that the little house where they now lived would one day be turned into a museum in honor of this very special baby. Wolfgang's second name was Theophilus, which means "loved by God." He liked to use the Latin translation of this name—Amadeus.

Leopold was a strict father, and he made sure his children worked very hard. But the family was a happy one, and all four Mozarts remained devoted to one another until they died.

Wolfgang Amadeus Mozart at about six years old. He is shown wearing special clothes for the royal court in Vienna. They were given to him by Empress Maria Theresa.

Wolfgang particularly enjoyed games and practical jokes, but he was also a keen pupil. By the age of five, he could play the harpsichord and violin like a professional, and had even begun to compose a few lines of keyboard music.

Leopold realized that his son was a **prodigy** and that fame and fortune were waiting for the boy. So he took time off from his own job to concentrate on teaching Wolfgang. He also began to plan grand tours of Europe, to show off the musical skills of both his children.

Wolfgang at the harpsichord, with his father and sister. The young genius had to be put on a high chair so that he could reach the keyboard.

Salzburg, in Austria, is right at the edge of the European mountain range known as the Alps. The center of this beautiful town has hardly changed since Mozart's day.

Wolfgang (at the harpsichord) plays background music for an elegant tea party. This sort of entertainment allowed **aristocrats** to talk to one another and walk around, while eating and drinking.

THE CHILD STAR

Mozart could hardly remember life before he became a star. From the age of six, he spent his childhood traveling around the noble courts of Europe, performing music alongside Leopold and Nannerl. The roads in those days were bumpy and slow. Traveling was difficult, and there were dangerous bandits about.

Despite this, Leopold managed to organize long and busy tours with his young family. They all suffered serious illnesses, but miraculously survived, and became the most fashionable music act in Europe. But Wolfgang never grew to be a strong man. His many illnesses left him small, pale, and delicate.

The Austrian Imperial family at Schönbrunn Palace. The Empress Maria Theresa (right) sits between her two elder sons, the future Emperors Joseph II (in red) and Leopold II.

The Mozarts' first important trip was to Vienna, capital of the **empire** and home of the imperial family, the Hapsburgs. Wolfgang played his instruments dressed as a miniature adult, with a sword at his side. He would perform amazing musical tricks, such as **sight reading** and **improvising** in different styles. He entertained the royal family at Schönbrunn Palace and amused the Empress Maria Theresa by asking one of her young daughters to marry him! She was Marie Antoinette, the future Queen of France.

In June 1763 the Mozarts left for Paris, stopping at many important towns and palaces on the way. They played for the King of France at Versailles, and Wolfgang published his first compositions. He was still only eight. They then moved on to London, where they became favorites of King George III and Queen Charlotte. Wolfgang particularly enjoyed his long stay in London. Here a scientific report was written about his extraordinary gifts, and he also met **J. C. Bach**, a famous composer. Young Mozart admired Bach's music and imitated his style.

An open-air concert in Vauxhall Gardens, London, typical of the sort that was popular when Wolfgang visited the city.

Their next destination was the Netherlands, and then finally back to Salzburg, stopping off in France, Switzerland, and Germany. By the end of 1766, after more than three years of traveling, they were home. Leopold had shown the world the miracle of his Wolfgang.

An example of rococo painting—*The Swing*, by Fragonard (1732–1806).

ROCOCO AND THE GALLANT STYLE

The music that Wolfgang played during his childhood belonged to what is called the gallant style. Music of the gallant style provided aristocrats with light entertainment. They would have tea, while musicians played graceful little tunes, full of delightful **ornaments**. The music was deliberately simple and easy to understand.

The gallant style was part of a larger **artistic movement** known as the rococo, which influenced painting, sculpture, and architecture, as well. A rococo painting, such as *The Swing* by Fragonard, usually shows a dream world full of love and fun. This was the age when men and women wore powdered wigs, delicate lace cuffs, and carried perfumed handkerchiefs. Art had to be pretty and entertaining.

Wolfgang later moved away from the gallant style and put more feeling and personality into his music. Some people thought this was unnecessarily complicated.

THE ITALIAN TOURS

Wolfgang did not settle in Salzburg for long. Leopold wanted his son to meet as many important people as possible while he was still young enough to impress them. So in 1767 they set out for Vienna again. This time they were unlucky. Wolfgang fell seriously ill with **smallpox**, and all concerts were canceled. He soon recovered, but his face was pockmarked for the rest of his life.

Mozart was used to uncomfortable traveling. He spent 14 of his 36 years away from home. He is shown here arriving in Florence with his father in 1770.

By 1768 Leopold realized that other musicians in Vienna were beginning to feel jealous of Wolfgang's brilliance. So he took his son instead to Italy, which at that time was the most important country in Europe for music. When they arrived in Milan, Wolfgang was asked to compose a full-scale **opera**. This was a great opportunity. The opera, *Mitridate, rè di Ponto*, was a triumph when it was performed in December 1770. Wolfgang **directed** it himself. He was 14 years old.

OPERA IN THE EIGHTEENTH CENTURY

In the eighteenth century, opera was more special than any other kind of music. When a composer was asked to write an opera, he knew that he had reached the top. During Mozart's life there were three different kinds of opera: *opera seria*, *opera buffa*, and *Singspiel*. *Opera seria* and *opera buffa* came from Italy and were always written in Italian. *Opera seria* used stories based on ancient Roman or Greek myths. These operas were serious and had a message about the victory of good over evil. They were usually commissioned for grand events, such as coronations. *Opera buffa* was comedy, and the characters would come from everyday life. *Singspiel* was completely different. It was like a funny musical pantomime, all in German. Dialogue was spoken rather than sung, the tunes were simple and catchy, and there were comic actors in the cast, as well as singers.

An eighteenth-century Italian *opera seria*. Although the singers are wearing eighteenth-century costumes, the story would have been set in ancient times. Wolfgang's early Italian operas looked much like this.

From Milan he traveled south to Florence, where he became good friends with another musical prodigy, an English boy called Thomas Linley. Linley was later drowned at the age of 22.

Wolfgang traveled on to Rome, where he visited the **Sistine Chapel**. He astonished his father by remembering and copying out, note for note, a choral work that he heard there. Until then the written music of this piece, Allegri's *Miserere*, had been a secret. While in Rome, the pope awarded him the Order of the Golden Spur, a very high honor.

The Mozarts visited Italy twice more over the next three years, hoping to find Wolfgang a permanent job in one of the royal courts there. But he was no longer a child, and the aristocracy were not as interested in him as before. The tours had brought him close to the music and musicians of Europe and had given him a wonderful education. But with no offer of a job, Wolfgang returned with his father to work in Salzburg.

Wolfgang is shown here wearing the Order of the Golden Spur.

RESTLESS IN SALZBURG

*L*eopold and Wolfgang found that life in Salzburg had changed. A new archbishop, a strict and unpopular man called Hieronymus Colloredo, had become ruler. Wolfgang was now officially a **Konzertmeister** at the archbishop's court, and Colloredo was determined to get his money's worth from him. So he was forced to settle down to work in Salzburg, which he found very boring after the excitement of his tours.

In 1774 the **Elector** of Bavaria asked Wolfgang to write an opera for the Munich carnival. Surprisingly, Archbishop Colloredo gave him permission to go. The opera, *La finta giardiniera*, was a huge success. Wolfgang was treated like a celebrity and went to endless parties. This made it all the more difficult to return to the dull routine in Salzburg. But over the next three years, he explored new ways of composing and soon found that he was expert at whatever kind of music he wrote.

Hieronymus Colloredo (1732–1812), who became Prince Archbishop of Salzburg in 1772.

Wolfgang's home in Salzburg. The Mozart family moved to this house in 1773, from the small apartment where Wolfgang was born. This photograph was taken in 1880, before the building was badly damaged by bombs during World War II.

Apart from opera, he composed brilliant violin **concertos**, **symphonies**, string **quartets**, **quintets**, **serenades**, and, even more importantly, piano concertos. Mozart was the first person to compose piano concertos as we know them today. They are like lively conversations between the piano and orchestra, which wander through different subjects and moods. He also had to write a lot of church music as part of his duties.

The archbishop was proud that Salzburg was becoming famous for its music. But he began to feel annoyed with the Mozarts, because they quite obviously did not like him and were always asking for permission to travel. In the end he let them go, but Leopold, afraid of losing his job altogether, decided to stay behind. So Wolfgang set off this time with his mother. It was September 1777, and he was now an adult of 21. For the first time in his life, he was free of his father's control.

A private performance of a harpsichord concerto. Mozart's early piano concertos were performed like this.

Small groups of musicians often met to play for pleasure in their own homes. This type of music is known as chamber music, and it includes serenades, quartets, and quintets.

HOPES AND DISAPPOINTMENTS

Leopold very much missed the company of his lively son but was determined that Wolfgang should find himself a good job. He sent letters full of stern advice. But Wolfgang was more interested in enjoying life. He knew he had to find work but was easily led astray by new ideas. He was also distracted by all the young women he met. One of the first was his cousin, Maria Anna Thekla, who lived in **Augsburg**. She shared his wicked sense of humor, and they became close friends.

Wolfgang and his mother then went north to Mannheim, where the court orchestra was supposed to be the best in Europe. He made many friends, and went to lots of wild parties, but failed again to find a job. Leopold was worried that he was wasting time and money. But the next piece of news made him furious. Wolfgang had fallen in love with a 16-year-old soprano called Aloysia Weber and wanted to take her to Italy. Leopold wrote immediately and persuaded his son to concentrate on earning a living. So in March 1778, Wolfgang said goodbye to the Webers and traveled on to Paris with his mother.

Wolfgang's young sweetheart, Aloysia Weber, later became a great opera singer. Although their relationship ended bitterly, Wolfgang wrote a great deal of music for her to sing, and eventually married her sister, Constanze.

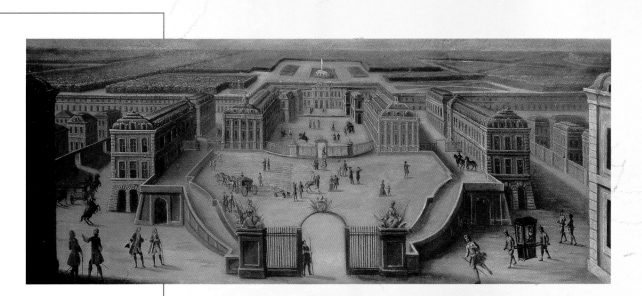

The palace at Versailles, in France. This enormous palace was built in the seventeenth century by the French king, Louis XIV. It became the king's home and the center of France's government. About 5,000 aristocrats, ministers, and servants lived within the palace. In 1778, Wolfgang was offered the post of organist at Versailles, but turned it down, ignoring the advice of his father.

He did not enjoy his stay in Paris. He thought the French were snobbish, and the French thought he was a showoff. Although he composed some brilliant works there, such as the Concerto for Flute and Harp, he had rivals who were determined not to let him succeed. One piece he wrote disappeared completely before it was even performed. Then his mother fell seriously ill and died on July 3. Wolfgang felt desperate.

Leopold realized the trip had been a disaster and begged Archbishop Colloredo to take Wolfgang back. He agreed, and offered the young man better terms than before, including more money and more freedom. Wolfgang had little choice but to return to Salzburg. He stopped off on his way home to see Aloysia, but was disappointed again. She had completely lost interest in him. He arrived home at last, depressed and ashamed, on January 16, 1779.

A
TURNING
POINT

The Mozart family, painted just before Wolfgang left Salzburg to live in Vienna. A portrait of Leopold's wife, who had died in 1778, hangs on the wall behind them. Nannerl's career as a musician ended with her childhood. She was married in 1784 and lived until 1829.

Munich, in Germany, where in 1780 Wolfgang's first great opera, *Idomeneo*, was staged.

Wolfgang was now appointed organist at the Salzburg court, which meant that he was expected to write more church music. In works such as his *Coronation* **Mass** we can see how skillfully he adapted his style to suit religious subjects.

Composing was as simple for him as writing words. He could work out clever new musical ideas more quickly and easily than other composers. This meant that his music was more sparkling and ingenious than anything people had heard before.

But Wolfgang wanted to write opera more than anything else. In 1780, a **commission** came out of the blue to compose an *opera seria* for the Munich carnival. He was given a story about the king of ancient Crete, Idomeneo, who returns home from the **Trojan War** to find all sorts of problems waiting for him. The opera was a great success. Wolfgang showed that he could create real characters and feelings out of music. It was his most brilliant work yet and marked an extraordinary turning point. After *Idomeneo* almost everything Wolfgang wrote, for the rest of his life, was a masterpiece. His musical education was complete.

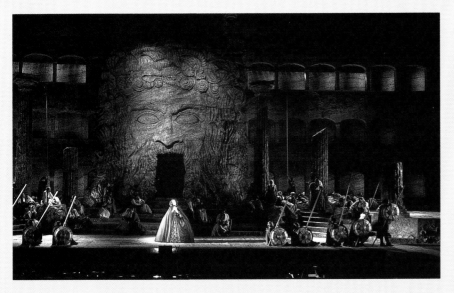

A scene from a modern production of *Idomeneo*. In the background the scenery includes a huge face—that of the Greek god Neptune.

Wolfgang's enjoyment of the Munich carnival was cut short by an order from his employer. He was to go and join Colloredo immediately in Vienna, to celebrate the **accession** of the new emperor, Joseph II. When Wolfgang arrived, he was treated like a lowly household servant. This frustrated him because he thought he deserved better. In Munich he had been admired and had made friends with many noblemen. He felt rebellious and started behaving rudely to Colloredo. A huge row followed, and in May 1781, Wolfgang was kicked out of the archbishop's service. It was another important turning point. Wolfgang was pleased to be free at last, but Leopold was horrified. There seemed less chance than ever that his son would settle down.

THE ENLIGHTENMENT

Mozart lived at a time when many people in Europe were beginning to resist old-fashioned, **oppressive** rulers. Writers such as **Voltaire** (1694–1778) and **Rousseau** (1712–1778) began to challenge the traditional powers of the Church and the aristocracy. They said that people would find true freedom only through understanding the laws of nature. Logic and science would wipe away tired old traditions and point the way to happiness for all.

This new way of thinking was later called the Enlightenment. It led to a great age of discovery, as brave explorers traveled far abroad in search of new peoples, countries, animals, and plants. One of the most famous of these explorers was Captain James Cook (1728–1779), whose three great journeys took him to the islands of the Pacific and the Antarctic.

The Enlightenment way of thinking led to political demands for equality and justice as several European countries prepared for revolution.

Captain Cook (1728–1779)

CONSTANZE

Much to his father's horror, Wolfgang now went to live with the Weber family, who had recently moved to Vienna. Aloysia was by this stage already married, but Wolfgang soon fell in love with Constanze, her 19-year-old sister. They were married in **St. Stephen's Cathedral** on August 4, 1782, despite Leopold's letters warning that it was a mistake. The marriage was a happy one, although Constanze outlived her husband by 50 years.

Wolfgang was beginning to earn a good living, although he still did not have a secure job. He was a **virtuoso** pianist as well as a composer, and he had a number of rich **patrons** who wanted to hear him play. This gave him the chance to perform his own music and arrange for it to be published. He also taught a few pupils. But the most important work he did during this first year in Vienna was to write another opera. *The Abduction from the Seraglio* is a *Singspiel* comedy, written in German, about a Spanish nobleman who rescues his lover from a Turkish **harem**. Turkey was seen as a very exciting place at that time in Vienna. Anything Turkish was fashionable, and the opera was an enormous success.

Constanze Weber (1763–1842), Mozart's wife, was also a fine singer, and he wrote several pieces of music for her. She was lively and shared her husband's sense of fun, but her health was delicate. She often had to leave Vienna for periods of rest. She married again 18 years after the composer's death and helped her new husband to write a book about Mozart.

Ouvre de MOZART

A scene from a modern production of *The Abduction from the Seraglio.* It shows the sort of Turkish costumes that in Mozart's day were considered very unusual and exciting.

In June 1783, Wolfgang and Constanze's first child was born. A few weeks later they left the baby with a nurse and set off on a visit to Salzburg. Their three-month stay there was difficult, because neither Leopold nor Nannerl approved of Constanze. To make matters worse, their baby died while they were away. It was to be the last time Wolfgang visited his home town.

Although work was going well for Wolfgang, he was beginning to have money problems. He spent more than he earned, he had an expensive apartment in the middle of town, and he liked to give big parties. But he told himself that the future would be fine and tried not to worry about money.

The center of Vienna, as Mozart would have known it. St. Stephen's Cathedral, where Mozart's wedding and funeral were held, is on the right, behind the street-front.

VIENNA'S FAVORITE

ozart was always busy at this time, giving concerts, teaching, composing remarkable new works, and staying out late with friends. By 1784 he was the talk of the town. But although he was happy, his health began to suffer, and in the summer he fell ill with a serious kidney infection. He was cheered up by the birth of a son, Karl. Only two of Mozart's six children survived, and Karl was one of them. He lived to be 74.

In December Mozart became a Freemason. Some of the empire's most important people were fellow Masons, including aristocrats, royalty, businessmen, and intellectuals. Mozart felt that he had been allowed into a very special private club, and that he had been accepted by Vienna's grandest society.

Leopold came to Vienna in February 1785 and was very proud of his son's success. He was there when Wolfgang played some of his string quartets to the great composer Haydn. Wolfgang had learned a lot from studying Haydn's music and wanted to honor the older man by dedicating the quartets to him. When the musicians finished playing, Haydn turned to Leopold and said, "Your son is the greatest composer known to me, either in person or by name."

Leopold was even more proud when he watched Wolfgang perform in front of the emperor. At the end Joseph II waved his hat and shouted, "Bravo, Mozart!"

Wolfgang was becoming more and more adventurous in his music. His concertos for **horn** show the happy side of his personality and are full of musical jokes. His new piano concertos were darker and more complicated. Different groups of instruments create contrasting effects, and the piano solo weaves around them, traveling through a whole range of moods.

In April 1785, Leopold returned to Salzburg, satisfied that his son was beginning a good career. Little did either of them know that they would never meet again.

Joseph Haydn who, after Mozart's death, became the teacher of another great composer—Beethoven.

Haydn

Joseph Haydn (1732–1809) was the other truly great composer of this period. Although Haydn was much older than Mozart, they became close friends and learned much from each other. Haydn was particularly good at writing for orchestra and also developed the string quartet more than any composer in the past. Wolfgang studied Haydn's music while developing his own style of orchestral and quartet composing.

Haydn spent most of his life working for the **Esterházy** family, who encouraged good music at their palaces. He soon became known as the most famous composer of his day. Toward the end of his life, he was given more freedom to travel and made two successful visits to England. He is remembered not just for his genius, but his kindness and loyalty as well. Like Mozart, he was also a Mason.

Freemasonry

Freemasonry is something between a men's club and a secret religion. In the Middle Ages it was like a **guild** for the stonemasons who built cathedrals. Then in the eighteenth century, Masons started to use ancient Egyptian and Greek symbols. New Masons had to go through traditional rituals and learn secret passwords. The centers where members assembled were called Grand Lodges. Mozart met many friends and supporters through Freemasonry and wrote several pieces of music for his Grand Lodge.

Freemasonry stood for brotherhood and friendship. Many of its members at that time also believed in freedom and the Enlightenment. Some of them may even have liked talking about revolution. This terrified politicians, who soon began to close down the Grand Lodges. By 1808, Freemasonry was illegal in Austria.

Mozart's Grand Lodge in Vienna. The blindfolded man in the middle is a new member being accepted into the Lodge. Mozart is sitting on the far right.

PARTNERSHIP
WITH DA PONTE

I n 1785, Mozart met a lively Italian poet called Lorenzo Da Ponte. They began working together on an opera, *The Marriage of Figaro*, based on a play by **Beaumarchais**. Da Ponte wrote the words. Their partnership is one of the most famous in the history of music.

The opera has a complicated story, in which an **immoral** count is fooled by his own servants.

Lorenzo Da Ponte (1749–1838)

Beaumarchais' play was banned in Austria, because the Emperor feared it might make ordinary people rebel against their rulers. But he allowed the opera to go ahead as long as Da Ponte made certain cuts to the story. Mozart and Da Ponte created a wonderful comic opera out of it, full of life and feeling. It has very realistic characters, who face very real problems. *Opera buffa* was now more than just something to laugh at.

Mozart and Da Ponte's next work was *Don Giovanni*. The story is about a charming but selfish **libertine**, who ends up being dragged to hell by the ghostly statue of a man he has murdered. This opera has everything: comedy, tragedy, romance, and horror. It was an instant success at its first performance, in Prague on October 29, 1787.

A scene from a modern production of *The Marriage of Figaro*. The count, seated on the left, has fallen into a trap laid for him by his servants Figaro and Susanna.

But in Vienna six months later, Mozart's enemies plotted to make sure the opera failed. They were envious of his talent and thought he was bad mannered. Among them was the famous court composer Salieri.

In 1789 the emperor asked Mozart and Da Ponte to work on another opera. They wrote *Così fan tutte*, a comedy about two men who disguise themselves and play a trick on their girlfriends. It has a serious message, too, about human weakness. Soon after *Così* was first performed, the emperor died, and Da Ponte left Vienna. He eventually went to New York, where he died nearly 50 years after writing his last opera with Mozart.

Mozart's main rival, the Italian composer Antonio Salieri (1750–1825), who wrote more than 40 operas.

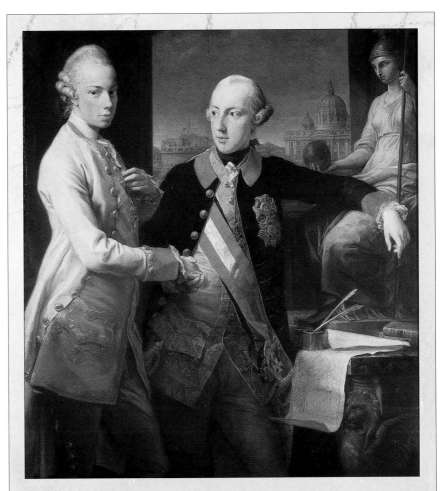

Emperor Joseph II (right) with his younger brother, Leopold, who succeeded him in 1790.

JOSEPH II
AN EMPEROR FOR THE PEOPLE

Joseph II (1741–1790) was a member of the Austrian royal family, the Hapsburgs. He was also called Holy Roman Emperor, a title handed down to Hapsburg rulers from medieval times. He was the son of the great Empress Maria Theresa, and he ruled with her until she died in 1780.

Joseph was a reformer who wanted to improve the lives of his people. He built hospitals, changed laws, accepted people of other religions, improved schools, encouraged the arts, allowed more freedom for the newspapers, stood up to the pope, and limited the power of the Church. He also put an end to **serfdom**. His reforms probably saved Austria from a revolution like the one in France, where in 1793 Joseph's sister, Marie Antoinette, was beheaded.

Outside Austria he was not so successful. His **subjects** in Hungary and the Netherlands were not happy with the reforms, and in 1788 he started an expensive war with Turkey. But many Austrians, including Mozart, were sad when he died. He was succeeded by his brother, Leopold II, who was far more old-fashioned.

HARD TIMES

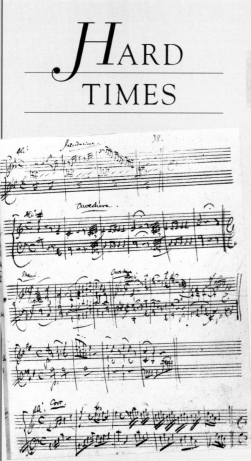

Mozart composed so much, he needed to catalog his work. In 1784 he began to copy down the opening of every composition. The page shown above includes six musical extracts.

Prague was the second most important city of the Austrian empire. Mozart's music was extremely popular there.

The years 1786–1789 were difficult ones for Wolfgang, despite the excitement of writing three new operas. His enemies in Vienna were powerful, and people seemed less interested in hearing his concerts. He also began to run into deep debt. In May 1787, his father died, and he lost the one person who truly understood his genius. He had not even had the chance to say goodbye. Some of his music from this period has a gloominess about it that was not there before. He wrote less for the entertainment of audiences and more to express his own inner feelings. This can be heard in his String Quintet in G minor, one of his greatest but most troubled works. On the other hand, he still composed bright and cheerful music, such as the popular *Eine kleine Nachtmusik*.

In November 1787, everything looked more hopeful. *Don Giovanni* was a triumph in Prague, and when Mozart returned to Vienna, he was offered the job of imperial chamber composer. But the pay was disappointing, and the job had very few responsibilities. Austria was also involved in an expensive war with Turkey, which meant that his former patrons now had less money to spend on music. Mozart's problems grew worse, and he was forced to move his family to a cheaper home outside Vienna.

A scene from the final act of *Don Giovanni*. The wicked Don is seen surrounded by devils as he is dragged down to the fire of hell.

Mozart had to start begging for money from fellow Masons. He always hoped to repay it but could find very little work and was still spending too much. One particular Mason friend, Michael Puchberg, was very generous and helped him on many occasions.

In April 1789, another friend, **Prince Lichnowsky**, offered to take Mozart to Berlin to introduce him to the **Prussian** king, Friedrich Wilhelm II. The king was musical and asked Mozart to compose some quartets. But there was no chance of a full-time job in Prussia, so he returned, poorer than ever, to Vienna.

The Bastille, a medieval fortress in Paris, was stormed on July 14, 1789. The Bastille held only seven prisoners at the time. But the storming marked the beginning of a revolution and is still celebrated each year.

THE FRENCH REVOLUTION

The mood in France during the 1780s was rebellious. The poor were starving, taxes were too high, and people were downtrodden by a rich aristocracy. King Louis XVI and Queen Marie Antoinette hardly seemed to notice the problem. But many writers of the period were standing up for people's rights. Jean Jacques Rousseau, for example, began his famous work, *Social Contract*, with the words, "Man is born free, but everywhere he is in chains."

In July 1789, the people of Paris rose up and stormed the Bastille, a prison-fortress and a symbol of royal power. The French Revolution had begun. A new parliament was set up, and at first the king was allowed to stay on with less power. But he tried to escape in 1791 to join his European allies, who were fighting to crush the Revolution. His plot failed, and he was brought back to an angry mob in Paris.

In 1792 the French **Republic** was declared, and the following year the king and queen were publicly **guillotined**. Over 40,000 French men and women were also executed in the next few years.

A scene from the film *Amadeus*. Mozart conducts one of his own operas in the candlelit theater. Emperor Joseph II, (dressed in a white suit) sits behind him.

$\mathscr{F}$ROM DESPAIR TO HOPE

When Joseph II died in February 1790, Mozart realized that he must win the favor of the new emperor, Leopold II. He applied for promotion at the court but was not offered anything better. In despair, he traveled to Frankfurt for the emperor's coronation, hoping to attract some attention with a concert. But although audiences enjoyed his music, the trip was disastrous because he failed to bring back any money. So he continued to beg from friends.

At the end of 1790, he was offered the chance to travel to England with Haydn. He refused because he didn't feel strong enough for the journey. Haydn was a good friend, and Wolfgang was in tears when they said goodbye. "I fear this is the last time we shall see each other," he said.

But life began to improve. He received some money for works that were being published, and he was offered the job of vice-**Kapellmeister** at St. Stephen's Cathedral. Then in July 1791, Constanze had their sixth child, Franz Xaver, and the baby survived. By this time an exciting new project was under way. Wolfgang had met an old friend and fellow Mason, the actor **Emanuel Schikaneder**, who asked him to compose a new comic opera in the German *Singspiel* tradition. Schikaneder had his own theater company. He would write the words of the opera and also take a leading role in it. *Singspiel* was very popular with ordinary people, and Wolfgang wanted to start right away.

Then, just as he was working harder than ever, two more commissions arrived. One was from a secret patron, who asked Wolfgang to write a **requiem mass**. The other was for a new opera, to celebrate Leopold II's coronation as King of **Bohemia**, and it had to be ready in less than two months. Suddenly there was more work than he could possibly manage, but the opportunities were too good to miss. He accepted all three.

Mozart's sons, painted seven years after the composer's death. Karl Thomas (right) became a civil servant and died in Italy in 1858. Franz Xaver, who was only a baby when Mozart died, was a music teacher in Salzburg until his death in 1844.

The bird-catcher Papageno, from the opera *The Magic Flute*, written by Mozart and Emanuel Schikaneder. Papageno was the role taken by Schikaneder, and was designed more for a comic actor than a singer.

A portrait of Mozart, drawn in 1789. People who knew Mozart said that he was very proud of his thick fair hair.

REQUIEM

An unfinished painting of Mozart playing the piano. His friends said that of all the portraits of the composer, this looked most like him.

The scenery used for a production of *The Magic Flute* in 1816. The great temple of wisdom is set in the middle of a wilderness, and the background stars are ordered in neat lines. These were clear symbols of the Enlightenment at the time.

or the coronation, Wolfgang was asked to write a classical *opera seria*, set in ancient Rome, called *La clemenza di Tito*. The first performance was set for September 6, in Prague. Wolfgang wrote as he traveled and composed it in 18 days. But *La clemenza* was not a great success with the public. *Opera seria* was no longer fashionable.

Back in Vienna, Mozart finished his opera with Schikaneder. This was *The Magic Flute*, a fairy tale about a prince who sets out to rescue a maiden. It is full of catchy tunes and special effects, monsters and witchcraft. All this was especially popular at the time, and it was a huge success. Schikaneder played a funny feathered birdman, called Papageno. The story is full of symbols, all about Freemasonry and the Enlightenment. The main characters move from a world of dark wickedness to a world of light and wisdom.

Wolfgang was now exhausted and ill with a fever. The cold weather set in, and he began to have fits of vomiting. He became obsessed with finishing the requiem and had ghostly visions of his own death. He worked on with his pupil **Süssmayr**, dictating, composing, and sketching out the remainder of the piece.

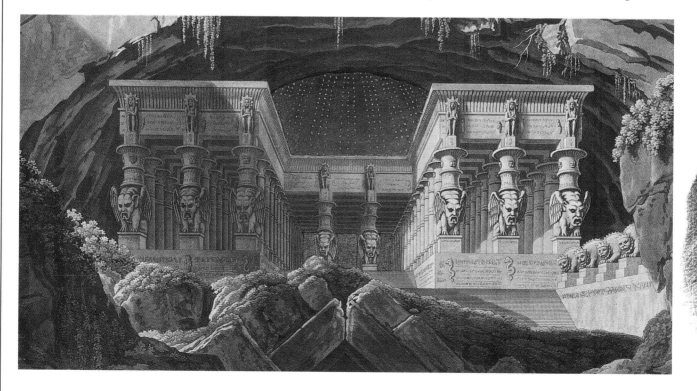

He became increasingly unwell, and on December 5, 1791, at one o'clock in the morning, he died. There was only enough money for the simplest of funerals. His body was taken out of town to be buried in an unmarked mass grave. To this day no one knows exactly where he lies.

In the years after Mozart's death, Constanze worked hard to get his music, including the requiem, performed and published. Soon the world realized the tragedy of what it had lost. There has never since been a story of quite such musical genius as that of Wolfgang Amadeus Mozart.

MOZART'S DEATH

No one, including the doctors, was really sure what caused the composer's death, and soon afterward rumors of murder began to be whispered around Vienna. Mozart had suspected that his enemies might be poisoning him. He also thought the mysterious man who had commissioned the requiem was a messenger sent from God to prepare him for death. Years later Salieri claimed that he had poisoned Mozart, but this was nothing more than the ramblings of a confused old man. Who was the requiem's secret patron? No one at all mysterious, as it turned out—just a local aristocrat who liked to buy music from composers and pass it off as his own.

The truth of Wolfgang's death is tragic, but not sinister. His childhood illnesses had left him physically weak. He was seriously ill in 1784, when his kidneys were damaged. The same symptoms of vomiting and fever returned in 1791, and the failure of his kidneys finally caused his death. The doctor's attempt to cool the fever by letting out blood only weakened him further.

He died in the company of Constanze and her sister Sophie. Constanze was so upset she crawled into bed with her dead husband so that she could catch his illness and die with him.

TIME CHART

1756 Wolfgang Amadeus Mozart born in Salzburg, January 27.

1762 First tour. Mozart plays for the Empress Maria Theresa in Vienna.

1763 Second tour, including five-month stay in Paris. First publication of music by Mozart.

1764 Arrival in England, where the Mozarts stay for 15 months.

1766 Returns to Salzburg.

1767 Goes to Vienna and falls ill with smallpox.

1769 Travels to Italy with Leopold in December (returning March 1771).

1770 *Mitridate, rè di Ponto* produced in Milan, December 26.

1771 Second tour to Italy, August–December.

1772 Third tour to Italy begins in October (returning March 1773).
Hieronymus Colloredo installed as Archbishop of Salzburg.

1775 *La finta giardiniera* produced in Munich, January 13.

1777 Leaves Salzburg to tour with his mother.
Falls in love with Aloysia Weber.

1778 Visits Paris where his mother dies, July 3.

1779 Returns to Salzburg and the Archbishop's court.

1781 *Idomeneo* produced in Munich, January 29.
Summoned to Vienna by Colloredo.

1782 *The Abduction from the Seraglio* produced in Vienna, July 16.
Marries Constanze Weber, August 4.

1783 Visits Salzburg for the last time.

1784 Falls seriously ill with kidney failure.
Karl Thomas Mozart born, September 21.
Becomes a Freemason.

1785 Meets Lorenzo Da Ponte.

1786 *The Marriage of Figaro* produced in Vienna, May 1.

1787 *Don Giovanni* produced in Prague, October 29.
Leopold Mozart dies, May 28.
Appointed imperial chamber composer, December.

1788 War with Turkey begins (ends 1791).

1789 Travels to Berlin.
French Revolution begins.

1790 *Così fan tutte* produced in Vienna, January 26.
Emperor Joseph II dies, February 20.
Travels to Frankfurt for coronation of Emperor Leopold II.

1791 Franz Xaver Mozart born, July 26.
Travels to Prague for production of *La clemenza di Tito*, September 6.
The Magic Flute produced in Vienna, September 30.
Mozart dies, December 5.

GLOSSARY

accession The moment when a person becomes king or queen.

aristocrat Someone who has inherited power, money, and property from ancestors. An aristocrat usually has a title, such as duke or earl. In the past an aristocrat often had advisors and assistants who made up his court.

artistic movement The history of art and music is divided up into different eras or "movements," according to the styles and fashions popular at the time.

Augsburg The town in Germany where Leopold Mozart was born. Wolfgang had many relations there.

Bach, J. C. (1735–1782) German composer (and son of the famous composer J. S. Bach) who became popular in Italy and England. He taught music to members of the English royal family.

Beaumarchais, Pierre de (1732–1799) French playwright who wrote comedies attacking the aristocracy.

Bohemia A state in the northern part of the Austrian Empire. Prague was the capital of Bohemia.

commission An invitation from an employer to a composer to write a piece of music for an agreed price.

concerto A piece of music written for orchestra and solo instruments.

dialogue The spoken lines of a play or opera.

direct To direct a piece of music means much the same as to conduct one. But the person directing usually leads the orchestra with his or her own playing, on the violin or at the keyboard.

elector The title given to certain aristocratic rulers in the Holy Roman Empire.

empire The Austrian Empire at this time included large areas of central and eastern Europe, together with parts of northern Italy.

Esterházy A Hungarian aristocratic family. Several of its members were distinguished soldiers and patrons of the arts.

guild A group of people who all do the same job and help one another in difficult times.

guillotine A method of execution by which the victim's head is cut off by a sharp blade suspended between two posts. Also the name of the device used.

harem The part of a Middle Eastern house reserved for women. This sometimes included several wives.

horn A brass musical instrument designed in a circular shape. It is blown like a trumpet.

immoral Having no morals. Ignoring what most people think of as right and wrong.

improvise Compose music while actually performing it, rather than playing from memory or from written music.

Kapellmeister The chief musician at the court of a ruler or aristocrat.

Konzertmeister A senior professional musician employed at the court of a ruler or aristocrat.

libertine A person who thinks himself or herself above all rules. Libertines live only for their own pleasure and often deceive and treat others unkindly.

Lichnowsky, Prince Karl An influential aristocrat and talented amateur musician, who, after Mozart's death, went on to become a patron of Beethoven.

mass An important part of church worship in the Christian religion. Many composers have set the mass to music.

opera A musical drama in which the performers sing most or all of their lines. The music is just as important as the words in an opera.

oppressive A way of ruling that uses cruelty and injustice to control people.

ornaments Musical decorations added to tunes.

patron Somebody who supports an artist by providing money or employment.

prodigy A child with a rare and extraordinary talent.

Prussia A powerful state in northeast Germany ruled over by the Hohenzollern family.

quartet A piece of music written to be performed by four musicians.

quintet A piece of music written to be performed by five musicians.

requiem mass A mass (see above) adapted specially for funerals or memorial services.

republic A country that is governed by the people, or on behalf of the people, by others they have elected. A republic is not ruled by a king, queen, or any other ruler who has simply inherited power.

Rousseau, Jean Jacques (1712–1778) A French writer and thinker, who believed in political freedom. He tried to change people's attitudes to religion, education, and nature.

Schikaneder, Emanuel (1751–1812) A theater director, playwright, and actor, born in Germany.

serenade This means music that is written for the evening, but in Mozart's time it also referred to music written on a small scale for a band of wind instruments.

serfdom A system of renting land that meant that poor farmers and their families were virtually owned by their rich landlords.

sight reading Playing music at sight, reading it for the first time from the written notes.

Sistine Chapel The pope's private chapel in the Vatican, in Rome. It was built in 1480 and decorated by some of the world's greatest artists.

smallpox An infectious disease that brings on a rash of spots. These often leave scars for life.

St. Stephen's Cathedral A huge church in the center of Vienna, built between 1300 and 1433. It is famous for its tall spire, which towers above the city.

subjects The people of a country who are governed by a king, queen, or other ruler.

Süssmayr, Franz Xaver (1766–1803) A Viennese composer who helped to complete the requiem after Mozart's death, and went on to become quite a successful composer.

symphony A piece of music written for orchestra.

Trojan War In the thirteenth century B.C., several Greek kings joined forces to fight a war against the city of Troy (in modern Turkey). The Trojan War, as it is called, has been an important source of legends ever since.

virtuoso A particularly skillful performer on his or her chosen instrument.

Voltaire, François (1694–1778) A leading French author of the Enlightenment. He was known for his humor and his lifelong fight against the injustice of oppressive rulers.

INDEX